A Time for Leaving

Mary Fahy

ILLUSTRATIONS BY
John Inserra

Paulist Press
New York/Mahwah, N.J.

Cover and book design by Lynn Else
Cover illustration by John Inserra

Library of Congress Cataloging-in-Publication Data

Fahy, Mary, 1938–
A time for leaving / Mary Fahy ; illustrations by John Inserra.
    p. cm.
ISBN 978-0-8091-4496-9 (alk. paper)
1. Hope—Religious aspects—Christianity. 2. Parables. I. Title.
BV4638.F34 2007
242—dc22

2007007029

Published by Paulist Press
997 Macarthur Boulevard
Mahwah, New Jersey 07430

www.paulistpress.com

Printed and bound in the
United States of America

To my parents,
Bernard and Geraldine,
who chose to trust,

and to all those who,
by entrusting their stories to me,
have shaped this book
with their lives.
M.F.

to my mother

the first artist
who shared with me
the way
j.i.

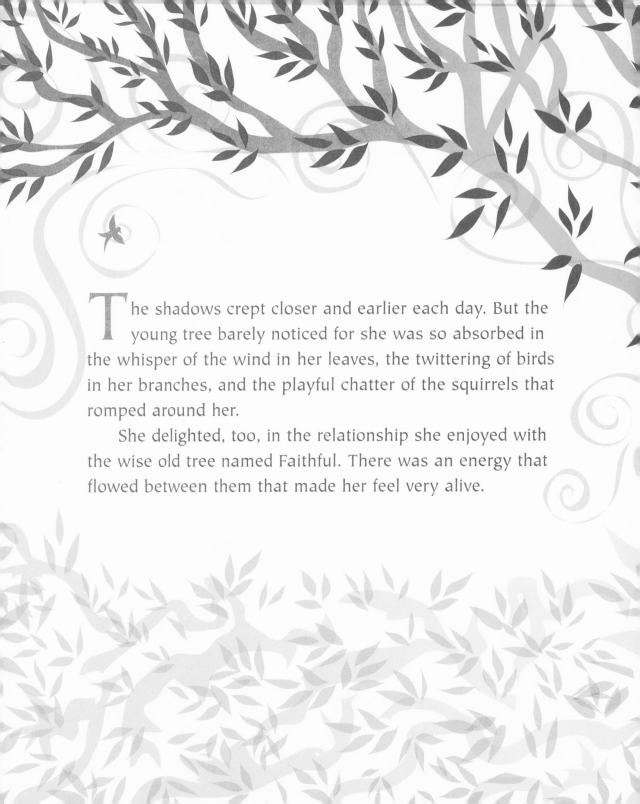

The shadows crept closer and earlier each day. But the young tree barely noticed for she was so absorbed in the whisper of the wind in her leaves, the twittering of birds in her branches, and the playful chatter of the squirrels that romped around her.

She delighted, too, in the relationship she enjoyed with the wise old tree named Faithful. There was an energy that flowed between them that made her feel very alive.

She loved hearing how she had surprised Faithful when she sprouted up next to her. She loved that Faithful had named her Joy. She loved her life. And she loved the fact that her leaves were beginning to change to a deep golden color.

It was a day in late summer, as the two were reminiscing, that Joy first noticed a scarlet leaf scuttle along the ground, chased by a feisty breeze.

"What's that?" she exclaimed.

"Oh, that's a maple leaf—probably from the grove around the corner," Faithful replied.

"It's very beautiful," said Joy. "But what is it doing here? Look! There are more!" As she spoke, other brightly colored leaves swirled playfully into view.

It's beginning," mused Faithful, and her voice trailed off, laden with the weight of memories.

"What's beginning? What's happening?" Joy demanded. "Those leaves don't belong on the ground. They belong on the tree."

"No," replied Faithful. "They don't belong on the tree anymore. They did for a while, but it is time for them to go. We call it the Leaving."

The Leaving? You mean they leave the tree? For how long?" There was a shrillness in Joy's voice that betrayed the panic she was feeling. "Did the tree do something wrong? Is he being punished? Is he sick or dying?"

"Nothing like that," said Faithful. "We all lose our leaves each year. It is our season of letting go."

Joy was stunned into a rigidity that even the winds teasing her branches could not revive. What was happening to her world? She had never been so happy, so beautiful, so full. And now she was being told that this would change?

Finally she whispered, "I don't want that to happen. I love my leaves. I would never let them go."

Just then a weary couple approached Faithful and traced their fingers over the initials they had carved on her trunk so many years before. But there was none of the exuberance they had previously felt. It had been replaced by emptiness and pain. Also missing was their son, who had so often joined them on the walks in the meadow.

"You have to let him go, Honey," said the wife.

Great sobs racked the man as he leaned against Faithful and cried out his anguish.

"I won't!" he cried. "It's not fair. He's so young. And I love him so much. I won't. I can't..."

Faithful supported him gently and encouraged his tears.

When he had finished crying, she let a leaf flutter to his feet. He picked it up and caressed it thoughtfully. After a long time, he took his wife's hand and headed slowly back into town. In his other hand he clutched the leaf, which seemed to give him new strength.

J oy was silent for a long time. Finally she said, "You gave him one of your leaves. Did it hurt?"

"Only a little," said Faithful, "because I was not quite ready to let go of it. What I felt most, though, was love for my friends, and the desire to comfort them. All I could do was give them a part of me."

Joy pressed on. "What do you mean, you weren't ready to let go?"

"The leaves have been with me for a long time," Faithful said gently. "It is not easy to part with them, but it makes the letting go easier if we remember and celebrate what we have meant to each other."

Fear held Joy hostage. "I think I'll just keep mine!" she said. "I don't want to change a thing about my life. I might never be this beautiful or happy again." She shook her leaves in defiance, scaring the birds resting in her branches.

Just then, a scowling woman trudged by, clutching a child roughly in each hand. The furrows in her face had been carved by years of anger and bitterness.

Faithful sighed. "That woman has never learned to let go. As a child she was treated very poorly. Since then, she has been unable to forgive or to trust anyone. That burden affects her life in many ways, and blocks out every message of love. Sadder still, she is passing this misery on to her children."

W hy didn't you give her a leaf?" Joy wondered aloud.

"I would if it would do any good," said Faithful. "But she is too blinded by bitterness to receive them. She would be so much happier if she could forgive, but it is hard, as she holds onto hurts like a shield against life."

Faithful paused, and Joy waited in silence.

"I think we are blessed by the rhythms of our year," Faithful said at last. "We may not always be ready, but it is necessary for us to let go of one season in order to welcome the next. The weight of snow on leaves is a heavy burden."

W hat about the oak trees?" argued Joy. "I remember seeing old brown leaves on their branches in the springtime."

"Ah yes! They are a mighty stubborn family," laughed Faithful. "Their leaves hang on tenaciously until spring buds come to push them off. When all others stand in graceful nakedness, the oaks are burdened with their stubbornness."

"Stubborn, nothing!" bellowed the majestic oak. "It's a matter of principle. It's a family tradition. Nothing takes my leaves away. And as for letting go willingly, choosing to trust, I find that most naive. I'll hang on to what I have until something better comes along."

H e sounds angry," said Joy, lowering her voice so as not to offend him further.

"I suspect it is more fear than anger," said Faithful. "It is scary for each of us to let go and open ourself to the unknown. The oak family has always believed more in security than risk."

"It's not only scary, it's stupid!" Joy startled herself with this latest declaration and glanced up warily at the older tree. "I think he's the smart one, and I agree with him! Besides, how do you know that spring will come again?" she demanded.

I remember the year I thought that I would never see another springtime," said another voice. It was the flowering cherry tree, speaking with a bit of hesitation.

"What happened?" Joy and Faithful asked in unison.

"One year in late summer," said the cherry tree, "we were surprised by a fierce hurricane. It whipped around us, bringing pelting rains and intense winds. It was the worst experience of my life.

"At first, I felt grateful to be alive. Numbness protected me from the full impact of the devastation, but when I saw that many of my friends had become uprooted or had lost their limbs, I began to feel a deep sadness."

Then I realized that I too had been hurt—my branches had snapped and my leaves were blown off. I had been stripped, and felt utterly confused and very angry. My inner turmoil was as bad as the outer had been, and I realized that I was scarred on the inside as well as the outside. I was so devastated that I just wanted to die."

"But you are lovely and strong today!" said Joy.

"Yes, but it took several years," the cherry tree replied. "The first spring, a few brave buds peeked out. I scolded them for being so silly as to trust again. But they insisted that they were obeying a voice within me that said, 'Live.' Despite myself, I began to heal in very small ways.

"I felt like a spectacle, though," she continued, "a big tree with only the merest of buds showing through. But the sun kept soothing me, and the other trees pleaded with me not to give up."

People who had admired my blossoms in past years started coming to see me again. They hugged me and said how happy they were to see me choosing life."

"But by the next spring you were beautiful again!" said Joy, hoping for a happy ending.

"Not quite," said the cherry tree. "It helped that the trees around me were going through the same thing. At first we hid our pain as if in some conspiracy of silence, but once we shared our experiences with each other, we began to feel more alive.

"We discovered, too, that we had each grown in ways that amazed us."

I s it hard to let go of your leaves after all you've been through?" asked Joy.

"I have learned that it is easier for me to participate in life's changes than to resist them," said the cherry tree. "We cannot always choose them, but we can decide how we will respond to them. Believe me, Little One, it is better to let go when it is time. Your friend Faithful is a wonderful example of someone who has learned to let go gracefully."

Faithful blushed, heightening the beauty of her crimson appearance.

"I have seen enough seasons to give me reason to trust," she said to the cherry tree. And then to Joy, she said, "You still have many experiences ahead that will make you even stronger and more beautiful than you are now. The Leaving is one of them, and it is time to prepare yourself for it."

Even if I don't want to?" Joy's voice began to quaver, her branches sagged, her leaves drooped, and heaviness dominated her whole being. "You sound as if you want it to happen," she challenged angrily.

"Part of me is sad," admitted Faithful, "but another part feels relieved for it is time to lay down my burden of fruitfulness."

"Burden?" Joy was incredulous. "I never knew you considered fruitfulness a burden. You seem so happy to be giving to others."

"I love being fruitful," her friend said, "but I also need a time when I can stand stark against the sky and just be me— not for my shade or beauty or nurturing. I need to feel the sun and rain directly, not as they filter through my leaves.

"The leaves stretch me to grow, but they also weigh me down. When the wind blows, they pull me in all directions. I love them, but I need a season to be without them."

Even as Faithful spoke, she realized how much she actually longed for winter. She wondered when she had changed.

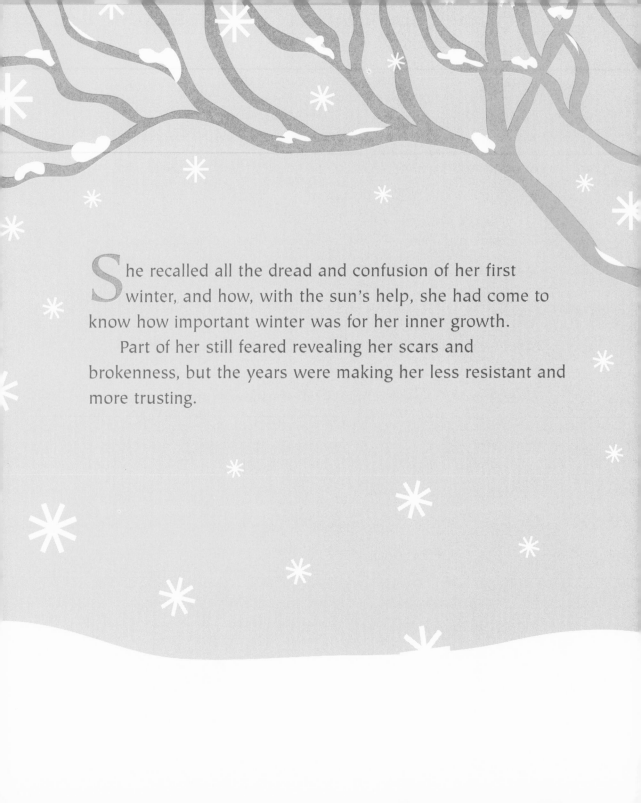

She recalled all the dread and confusion of her first winter, and how, with the sun's help, she had come to know how important winter was for her inner growth.

Part of her still feared revealing her scars and brokenness, but the years were making her less resistant and more trusting.

She remembered her old friend the elm. His days had numbered more than hers. Then there came a day in late fall when he said farewell to the trees and spoke of a time when he would see them again in some eternal springtime. Faithful knew she was not ready to join him, but she also knew that with each passing season, the thought held less fear.

"I've been changing," she thought to herself. "With your help!" she whispered to the sun.

B ursting through a passing cloud, the sun kissed each tree tenderly and acknowledged, "Love does wonderful things."

Faithful sighed happily because these encounters enlivened her spirit. "Knowing I am loved enables me to say yes," she said to Joy. "And you, too, are very much loved—by the sun and by the rest of us as well."

"I know," whispered the sapling shyly. "I feel the sun's love, especially through you."

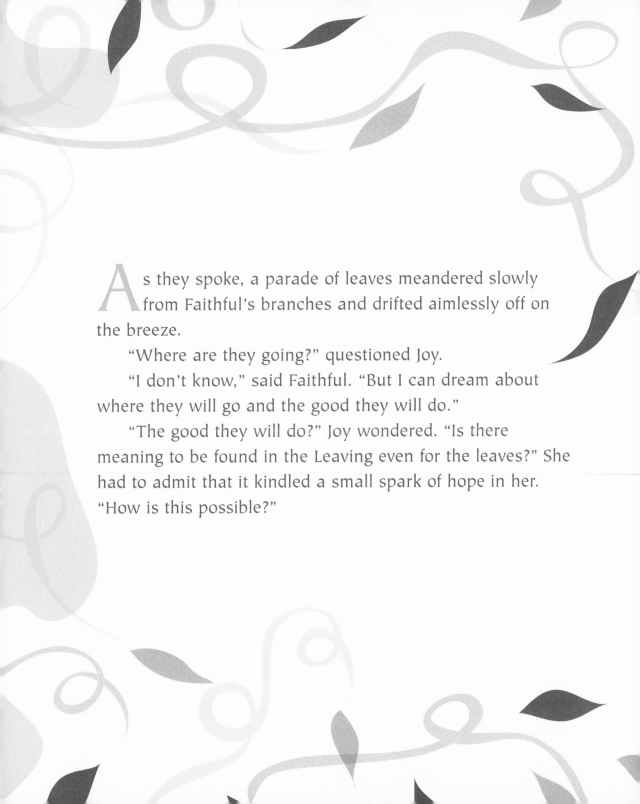

As they spoke, a parade of leaves meandered slowly from Faithful's branches and drifted aimlessly off on the breeze.

"Where are they going?" questioned Joy.

"I don't know," said Faithful. "But I can dream about where they will go and the good they will do."

"The good they will do?" Joy wondered. "Is there meaning to be found in the Leaving even for the leaves?" She had to admit that it kindled a small spark of hope in her. "How is this possible?"

Some of my leaves will join the earth and provide it with rich moist soil," Faithful explained. "Others will provide protection for plants and animals during cold spells. Many kept us warm last winter.

"But I think the most good comes at the actual moment of letting go, when I am most in harmony with the rest of nature and know within me that I am part of a plan that is greater than I can understand."

With great reluctance, Joy finally said, "Well, maybe I'll let go of one or two, just to see how it feels."

She selected a couple of leaves that were well hidden from view.

"Now!" she commanded. "You can go now!"

Nothing happened! She stretched and squeezed and pushed. Still nothing happened! She held out the leaves so that the next wind would carry them away. Again nothing happened! In frustration, she shook them vigorously, but they would not budge.

I'm afraid it doesn't work that way," explained Faithful. "Letting go is not something that is entirely up to you. You cannot just make it happen. All you can do is allow it, and then wait.

"There were times when some of my leaves held on and refused to let go," said the older tree. "They needed to be reassured that I was not rejecting them."

"Hmmm…," murmured the younger tree, as she felt the familiar tug of her own leaves dancing in the wind. She understood the strong bond that existed between her leaves and herself. Yet she was beginning to understand that nature had a certain wisdom. Despite this, she was still far from wanting the Leaving to happen to her.

O n that distant hill, where it is colder and windier," Faithful continued, "the ash tree has already lost most of her leaves. But it is evident by her stiffness that she did not let go willingly. She is the picture of brittle resentment. She refuses to let go of her memories, or of how she wanted life to be."

"Do you mean I have to let go of my memories too?" Joy was understandably baffled. "Is it wrong to remember my summer fun?"

"Memories are wonderful," reassured Faithful, "unless they become more important than living. It will be difficult for new buds to form on the ash tree if she holds herself so stiffly that spring energy cannot flow freely in her."

"That is very sad," said Joy. "Will she die?"

"Probably not, but spring will not find in her the welcome it deserves, nor will she recognize those early signs of quickening. To miss even a moment would be such a waste."

Joy sank into a deep reflective silence while Faithful stood by, reverencing her struggle.

"I want to trust," said Joy, amazed by her own words. "Will you help me let go when the time is right?"

As she spoke, she sensed a new freedom in herself. Where had it come from? She glanced up in time to see the sun winking at her.

"Something happened!" she said to Faithful. "All of a sudden I feel lighter and more peaceful. And I haven't lost a single leaf."

"But you did let go of something," said Faithful wisely. "You let go of how you thought things should be. And you asked for help. That is something to be celebrated!"

They entwined their branches affectionately as the sun painted the sky in festive colors for the occasion.

Faithful began swaying gently. "Feel how freeing it is to move in harmony with nature."

"Oooh!" Joy sighed, feeling her resistance yield to relaxation. "This feels better than fighting to hold on."

Faithful continued, "Now allow yourself to let go. Release your leaves from any expectations, and allow them to go when they want."

"If you say so," said Joy, surrendering in trust. "Is that all?"

"Now you wait for the moment of grace," said Faithful. "Sometimes it comes as an invitation from another. And sometimes it comes as an inner conviction that it's time. Trust, my friend, and you will know."

Some days found Joy feeling courageous and open to mystery. Others brought doubt, hesitation, and fear. But as she watched the sun set each day, she kept repeating, "I choose to trust."

One day, a group of children came to the meadow, tumbling in the multicolored leaves.

"They're pretty!" exclaimed a small boy. "I'm going to bring some to my friend. She's too sick to go out." He looked up at Joy and said, "I wish I had some of those yellow leaves, too!"

Before she had time to think, Joy said, "Here, have some!" With that, some of her golden leaves floated toward the ground. The boy was elated, but his happiness was greatly exceeded by what Joy was feeling.

"What happened?" asked Joy, bathed in a euphoria she had never known before.

"You've just experienced an important passage," said Faithful. "You have moved from simply letting go to giving. I am so very happy for you."

"Why didn't you tell me it would feel like this?" puzzled Joy.

"Because not all Leavings feel like that," Faithful said. "Sometimes you feel lonely, scared, or even angry. It is part of grieving what has been precious to you. But these feelings are your friends. Honor them and learn from them. If the Leaving is truly right, you will have another feeling, too. Deep down you will be at peace."

"I feel that now," whispered Joy. "And another thing—I feel sort of grown up."

"You have grown a great deal today," said Faithful. "There are many more lessons that can be learned only by living. Don't be afraid to live."

Together they watched as the child scampered off with his bouquet of leaves. Joy nudged the older tree and pointed in his direction.

"Look! What he holds is part of you and part of me. We have helped to create something new."

"Yes," affirmed Faithful. "Just like the gift we all give together as we blanket the earth with our leaves."

The sound of children reverberated in the air and then disappeared in the distance. In its place all that could be heard was the whisper of the wind and the rustle of crimson and golden leaves as they fell in graceful benediction upon a grateful Earth.

All was as it needed to be. And the world was one step closer to peace.